The 21st Century Guitar Method

GUITAR THEORY 2

CONTENTS

Photography: Roberto Santos

Alfred

ISBN 0-89898-897-7 (Book)

Note Review

Name the notes, notate them in the tablature, then play them:

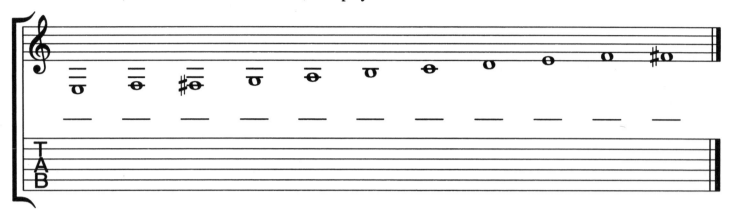

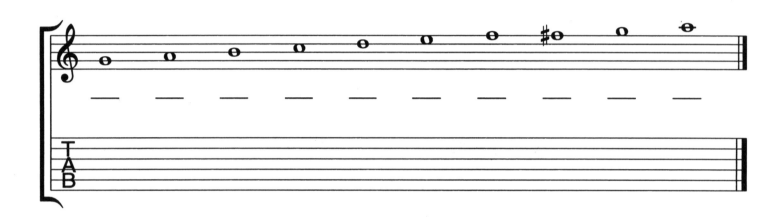

Rhythm Review

Add the bar lines, then clap the rhythm:

Chord Review

Name the chords, then play them:

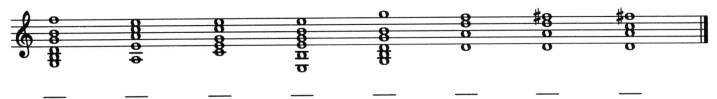

Name the power chords, then play them:

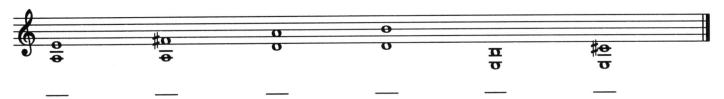

Sharps Review

A **sharp** sign (♯) raises the pitch of a note one half step.

When saying a sharp note's name, we say the letter name first and the sharp next—F sharp. When we write it on the music, the sharp sign comes first, centered on the same line or space as the note.

To draw a sharp, draw two vertical lines:

Then add the slanted lines:

Draw sharps before both F's:

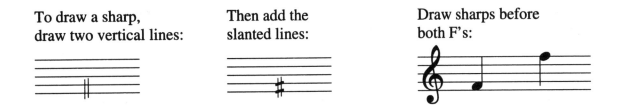

Name the indicated notes:

Draw the indicated notes:

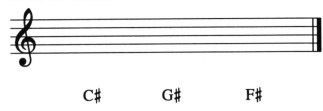

C♯   G♯   F♯

Use after page 3 of Belwin's 21st Century Guitar Method 2.

The Key of C contains no sharps.
Name the notes of the C scale:

_ _ _ _ _ _ _ _ _ _ _ _ _ _

Each fret on the guitar neck equals one half step.

If we start at C and go up the guitar neck, we see that all of the tones in the C scale are separated by a whole step with the exception of E to F and B to C, which are half steps.

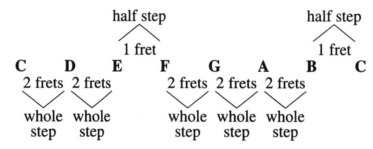

The pattern of whole and half steps is easy to see when playing the scale on one string.

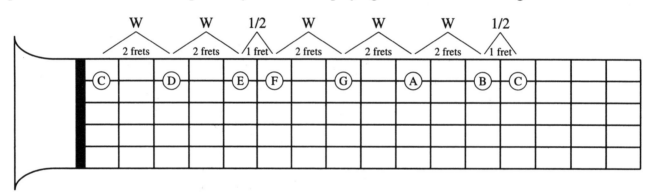

Name the notes of the C scale:

_ _ _ _ _ _ _ _ _ _ _ _ _ _

Indicate if the distance between the two notes is a whole (W) or half (1/2) step.

W   _   _   _   _   _

Use after page 5 of *Belwin's 21st Century Guitar Method 2.*

When playing the C scale on the B string you move from first position, to fifth position to tenth position. Add the correct fret numbers in the tablature.
Remember W = 2 frets, 1/2 = 1 fret.

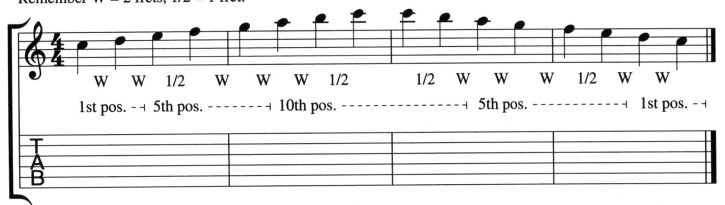

When playing the C scale incorporating the E string, you play the first two notes and last two notes on the B string and the rest on the E string. By doing this you only have to move from first position to fifth position. Add the correct fret numbers in the tablature.
The circled numbers are string indications: ② = 2nd string.

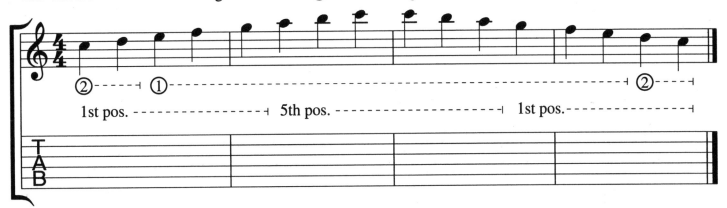

Draw the notes indicated on the fingerboard diagram, on the staff below.
Name the notes.

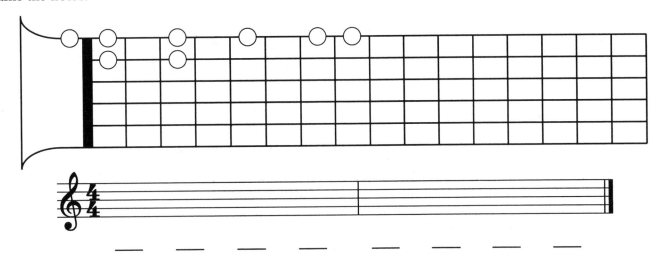

Use after page 5 of Belwin's 21st Century Guitar Method 2.

A chord's relationship to a key, and to other chords within that key, is indicated by numbering the chords from 1 to 7. The numbers are shown with Roman numerals.

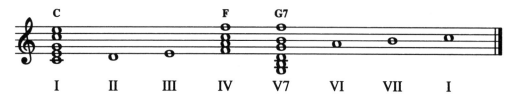

The chord built on the 1st degree of the C scale is the C chord, or I chord in the key of C.
The chord built on the 4th degree of the scale is the F chord, or IV chord in the key of C.
The chord built on the 5th degree of the scale is the G7 chord, or V7 chord in the key of C.
The I, IV and V7 chords are the most common chords (primary chords) in any key.

The C, F and G7 chords are illustrated on the chord frame diagrams. Draw the indicated notes on the music staff.

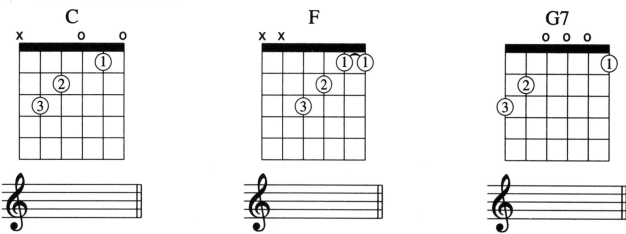

1. Notate, on the tablature, the chords indicated in the treble staff.
2. Name the chords and indicate the Roman numeral that shows their relationship to the key of C.

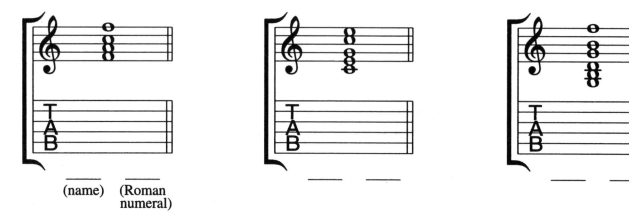

_____ _____
(name) (Roman numeral)

Use after page 6 of Belwin's 21st Century Guitar Method 2.

D.C. stands for the Italian phrase: *Da Capo* which means go back to the beginning.

Fine means the end.

D.C. al Fine means go back to the beginning and play to the end.

On the blank staff write the music as it would appear without using the D.C. al Fine.

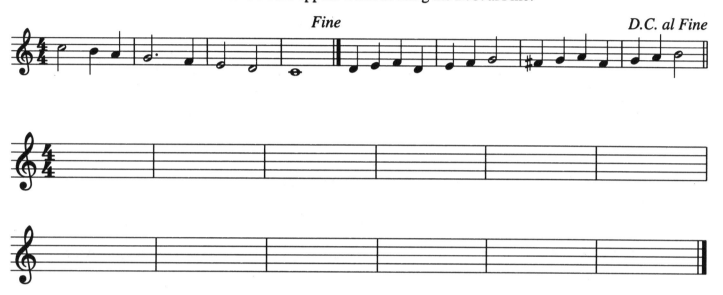

Fingerboard Review

Indicate on the fingerboard, the place where each note of the C scale would be played.

C Scale

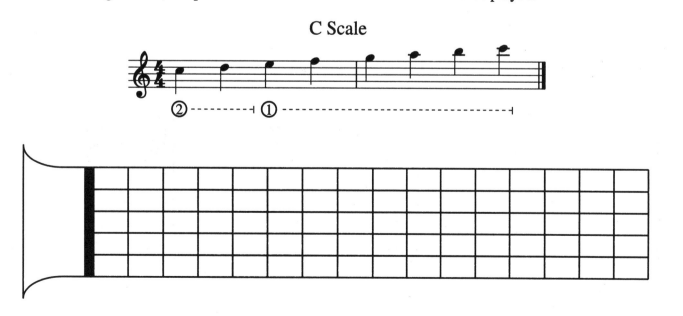

Use after page 9 of Belwin's 21st Century Guitar Method 2.

The I, IV and V7 chords are the most common chords in a key. The II and VI chords are the next most often used (secondary chords).

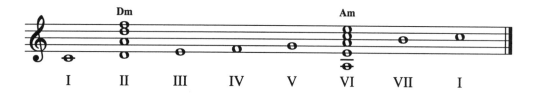

| I | II | III | IV | V | VI | VII | I |

The chord built on the 2nd degree of the C scale is the Dm chord, or II chord in the key of C. The chord built on the 6th degree of the scale is the Am chord, or VI chord in the key of C.

1. Notate, on the tablature, the chords indicated in the treble staff.
2. Name the chords.

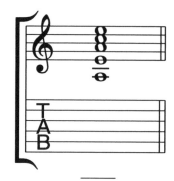

_____

_____

Fill in the chord frame diagrams to illustrate how the chords are fingered on the guitar fretboard and indicate the Roman numeral that shows their relationship to the key of C.

Dm

_____

Am

_____

Use after page 10 of Belwin's 21st Century Guitar Method 2.

Fill in the chord frame diagrams to illustrate how the chords are fingered on the guitar fretboard:

G7

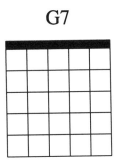

C

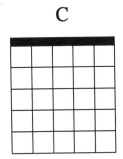

F

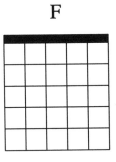

The Am and Dm chords are illustrated on the chord frame diagrams below. Fill in the notes on the music staff.

Am

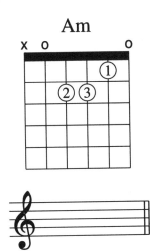

Dm

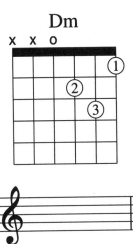

1. Write the chords indicated by the Roman numerals for the key of C.
2. Notate the chords on the tablature.

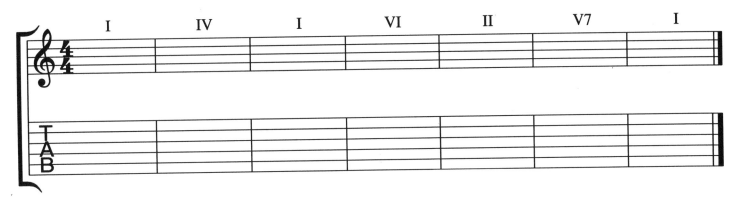

3. Name the chords and play them.

Use after page 10 of Belwin's 21st Century Guitar Method 2.

Dotted Quarter Note

A **dot** placed after a note adds one-half the value of the original note. A dotted quarter note (♩.) equals 1-1/2 counts.

Add bar lines in the appropriate places (every four beats). End with a double bar.

Add bar lines, then name the notes.

Add the beats:

♩ + ♪ + ♩. = ___ beats   ♩. + ♩ + ♪ = ___ beats

♩. + ♪ + ♩ = ___ beats   ♩. + ♩. + ♪ = ___ beats

Draw the note that equals the number of beats:

♩. + ♫ + ♩ =   ♫ + ♪ =

♫ + ♩. + ♪ =   ♩. + ♪ =

Complete the rhythms in the following measures. Use only one note in each.

Use after page 11 of *Belwin's 21st Century Guitar Method 2*.

A **flat** sign (♭) lowers the pitch of a note one half step.

When saying a flat note's name, we say the letter name first and the flat next—B flat. When we write it on the music, the flat sign comes first, centered on the same line or space.

To draw a flat, first draw the vertical line:

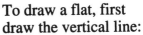

Then add a curve:

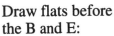

Draw flats before the B and E:

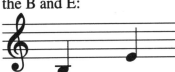

Name the indicated notes:

Draw the indicated notes:

B♭   E♭   G♭

A **natural** sign (♮) cancels the effect of a flat or sharp.

To draw a natural, first draw an ∟:

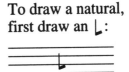

Then add another ⌐ upside down:

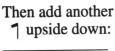

Draw naturals before both F's:

A natural is centered on the line or space it affects. Flats, sharps and naturals are called **accidentals.**

They affect every note on the same line or space for an entire measure.

A natural sign cancels the flat within the same measure.

A bar line also cancels an accidental.

When a note is tied across the bar line, its accidental carries across.

Name the indicated notes:

Use after page 13 of Belwin's 21st Century Guitar Method 2.

11

Key of G

The Key of G contains one sharp: F♯.
Name the notes of the G scale. Remember there is an F♯ in the key signature.

The pattern of whole steps and half steps in the G scale is the same as in the C scale and in all major scales.

Indicate if the distance between each note of the scale is a whole step (W) or half step (1/2).

Indicate on the fingerboard, the place where each note of the G scale (up to high E) would be played.

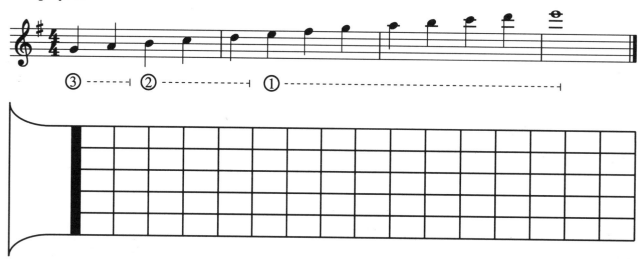

Name the notes and play them:

Use after page 17 of Belwin's 21st Century Guitar Method 2.

As we learned in the key of C, a chord's relationship to a key and to other chords within that key is indicated by numbering the chords 1 to 7 shown with Roman numerals.

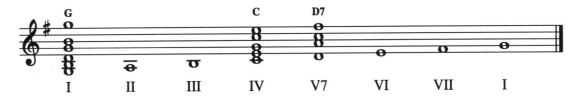

The chord built on the 1st degree of the G scale is the G chord, or I chord in the key of G.
The chord built on the 4th degree of the scale is the C chord, or IV chord in the key of G.
The chord built on the 5th degree of the scale is the D7 chord, or V7 chord in the key of G.

The G, C and D7 chords are illustrated on the chord frame diagrams. Draw the indicated notes on the music staff.

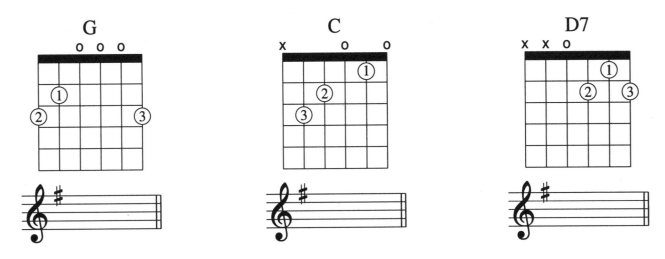

1. Notate, on the tablature, the chords indicated in the treble staff.
2. Name the chords and indicate the Roman numeral that shows their relationship to the key of G.

(name) (Roman
         numeral)

Use after page 18 of *Belwin's 21st Century Guitar Method 2*.

Secondary Chords in the Key of G

As we learned in the key of G, the two secondary chords in a key, the ones used most often after the I, IV, and V7 chords are the II and VI chords.

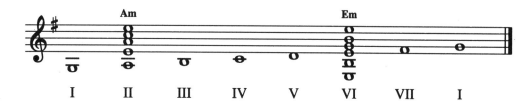

I	II	III	IV	V	VI	VII	I

The chord built on the 2nd degree of the G scale is the Am chord, or II chord in the key of G. The chord built on the 6th degree of the scale is the Em chord, or VI chord in the key of G.

1. Notate, on the tablature, the chords indicated in the treble staff.
2. Name the chords.

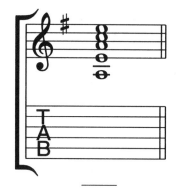

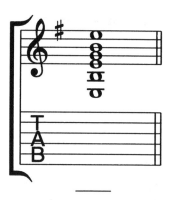

Fill in the chord frame diagrams to illustrate how the chords are fingered on the guitar fretboard and indicate the Roman numeral that shows their relationship to the key of G.

Em

Am

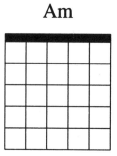

Use after page 19 of *Belwin's 21st Century Guitar Method 2.*

Fill in the chord frame diagrams to illustrate how the chords are fingered on the guitar fretboard:

D7

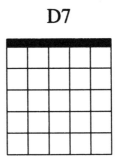

G

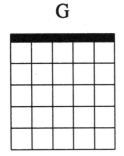

C

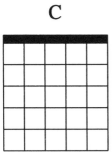

The Em and Am chords are illustrated on the chord frame diagrams below. Fill in the notes on the music staff.

Em

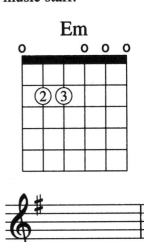

Am

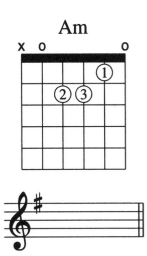

1. Write the chords indicated by the Roman numerals for the key of G.
2. Notate the chords on the tablature.

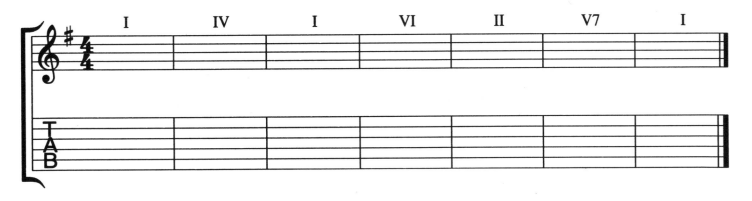

3. Name the chords and play them.

Use after page 19 of *Belwin's 21st Century Guitar Method 2.*

Syncopated rhythms, those that do not fall on the strong beats of the measure, add excitement to all styles of music.

Add the bar lines, then clap the rhythm:

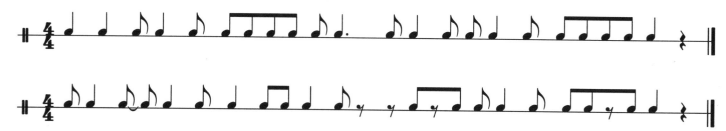

Rest Review

Fill in the blanks:

One whole rest equals _____ beats.
One quarter rest equals _____ beat.
One half rest equals _____ beats.

In the next exercise, fill in the missing beats with rests. Use only one rest in each measure, then clap the rhythm.

Add the bar lines, then clap the rhythm:

Rock Trivia

Fill in the composer credit.

The composer of *Margaritaville* was born in Mobile, Alabama on December 25th, 1946. He settled in Key West, Florida in 1971 and his music and lyrics reflect the relaxed lifestyle of the area. *Margaritaville* reached the position of 8 on the Billboard charts on May 7, 1977. Other Top 40 hits of this composer were *Come Monday, Cheeseburger in Paradise, Fins* and *Changes in Latitudes, Changes in Attitudes*. The composer is _____ _____ .

Use after page 23 of Belwin's 21st Century Guitar Method 2.

Before learning the moveable power chord shapes, you must familiarize yourself with notes on the low E and A strings. Although there are no new notes in the following exercises, many of the notes are in new positions.

Notate, on the tablature, the notes indicated on the treble staff.

Natural notes on the low E string:

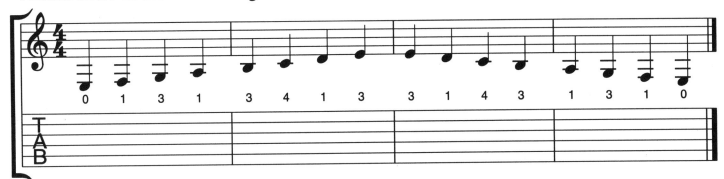

Natural notes on the A string:

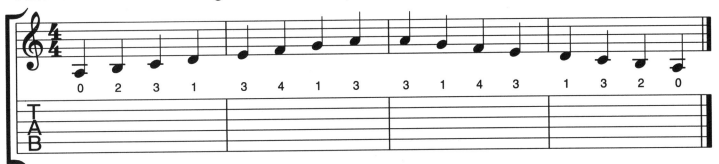

Power chords with the root on the sixth string (root ⑥):
The lowest note in each chord (played by the first finger) is the root. The number on the right of each frame (3fr., 5fr. etc.) shows the fret at which the chord is played.

Name the chords, then play them.

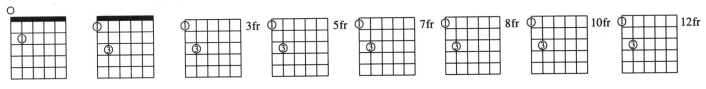

Power chords with the root on the fifth string (root ⑤):
The chord shapes will be identical to the root ⑥ form. Remember the root is still located under the first finger.

Fill in the chord frame diagrams to illustrate how the chords are fingered on the guitar fretboard, then add the fret numbers to show where they are played.

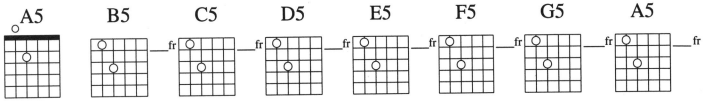

Use after page 24 of Belwin's 21st Century Guitar Method 2.

The power chords with the root on the fifth string (root ⑤) are illustrated on the chord frame diagrams.

1. Draw the indicated notes on the music staff.
2. Notate the chords on the tablature.
3. Play the chords.

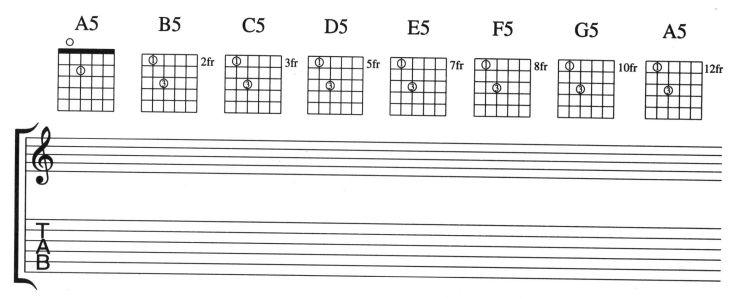

The power chords with the root on the sixth string (root ⑥) are illustrated on the chord frame diagrams.

1. Draw the indicated notes on the music staff.
2. Notate, on the tablature, the chords indicated.
3. Name the chords and play them.

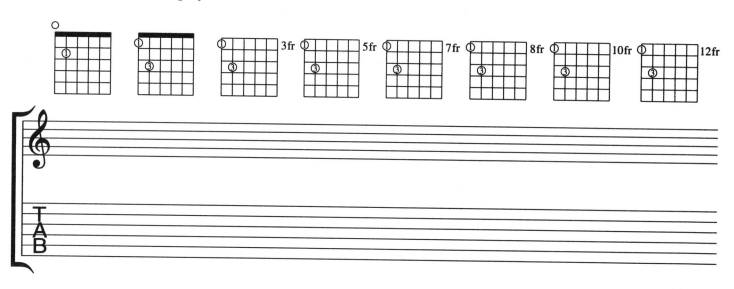

Use after page 25 of Belwin's 21st Century Guitar Method 2.

Cut time is basically a fast 4/4 time. The cut time signature (¢) actually means 2/2 time: Two beats in a measure, a half note gets one beat.

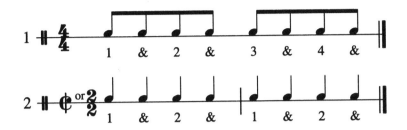

Using cut time makes it easier to read fast songs. It also changes the "feel" of the song since the counting is done "in 2" rather than "in 4."

Here are the first four measures of *The Entertainer.* In the space below write these four measures as they would appear in cut time.

Chord Review

Write the chords indicated in the key of C. Name the chords.

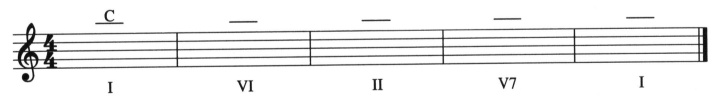

Write the chords indicated in the key of G. Name the chords.

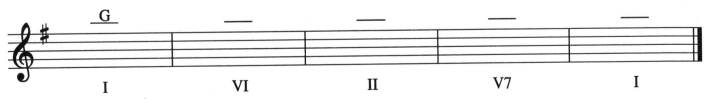

Use after page 29 of Belwin's 21st Century Guitar Method 2.

Triplets: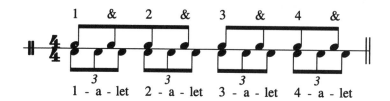

A triplet is a group of three notes played in the space of two of the same value.
The eighth note triplet is the most common triplet figure.

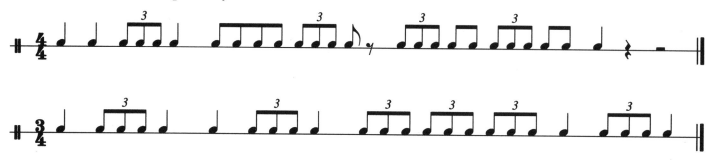

Add the barlines, then clap the rhythm:

Add the beats:

𝅘𝅥 + 𝅘𝅥𝅘𝅥𝅘𝅥³ = ___ beats   𝅘𝅥𝅮𝅘𝅥𝅮 + 𝅘𝅥𝅘𝅥𝅘𝅥³ = ___ beats

𝅗𝅥 + 𝅘𝅥𝅘𝅥𝅘𝅥³ = ___ beats   𝅗𝅥. 𝅘𝅥𝅮 + 𝅘𝅥𝅘𝅥𝅘𝅥³ = ___ beats

Draw the note that equals the number of beats:

𝅘𝅥𝅘𝅥𝅘𝅥³ + 𝅘𝅥 + 𝅗𝅥 =   𝅘𝅥𝅘𝅥𝅘𝅥³ + 𝅗𝅥. 𝅘𝅥𝅮 =

𝅘𝅥𝅮𝅘𝅥𝅮 + 𝅘𝅥𝅘𝅥𝅘𝅥³ + 𝅘𝅥 =   𝅘𝅥𝅮𝅘𝅥 𝅘𝅥𝅮 + 𝅘𝅥𝅘𝅥𝅘𝅥³ =

Complete the rhythms in the following measures. Use only one triplet in each.

Use after page 30 of Belwin's 21st Century Guitar Method 2.

20

In Book One we learned the power chords for the boogie pattern in A. To play the boogie pattern in E we must first review the B5 chord and learn the B6 chord.

The B5 and B6 power chords are illustrated on the chord frame diagrams. Draw the indicated notes on the music staff.

B5

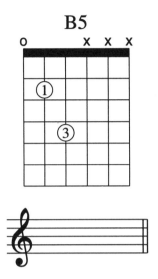

B6

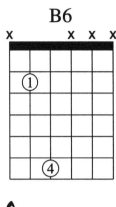

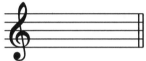

1. Notate, on the tablature, the chords indicated in the treble staff.
2. Name the chords.

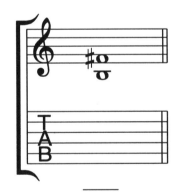

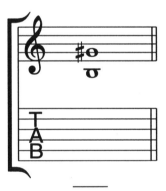

_____

_____

Fill in the chord frame diagrams to illustrate how the chords are fingered on the guitar fretboard:

B6

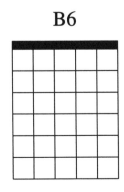

B5

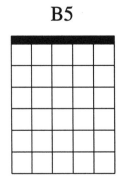

Use after page 33 of Belwin's 21st Century Guitar Method 2.

A shuffle is usually indicated by this symbol: (♪♪ = ♩³♪)
Remember: All shuffles use the uneven eighth note rhythm (long-short-long-short).

The Blues Shuffle alternates between the power chords (E5, A5 and B5) and the power sixth chords (E6, A6 and B6). Fill in the chord frame diagrams to illustrate how the chords are fingered on the guitar fretboard. Then follow the rhythm slashes and play *The Blues Shuffle*.

The Blues Shuffle

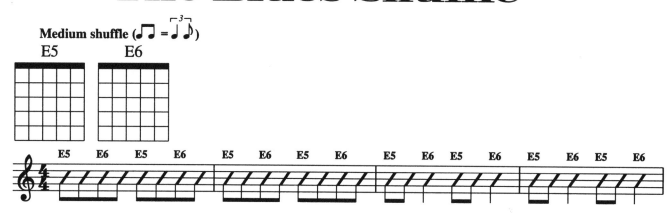

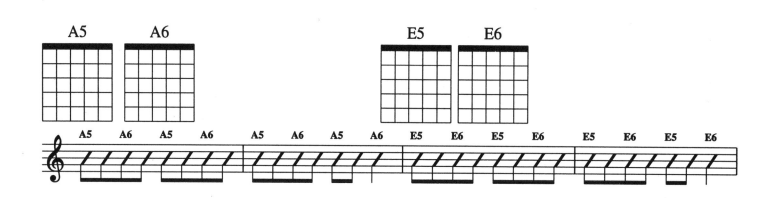

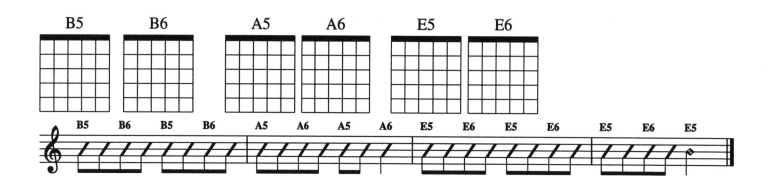

Use after page 33 of *Belwin's 21st Century Guitar Method 2*.

The two-note power 7th chord is a natural extension of the power 5 and 6 chords.

The E7, A7 and B7 power chords are illustrated on the chord frame diagrams. Draw the indicated notes on the music staff.

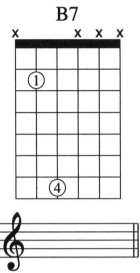

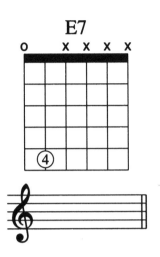

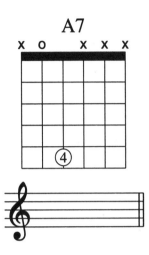

1. Notate, on the tablature, the chords indicated in the treble staff.
2. Name the chords.

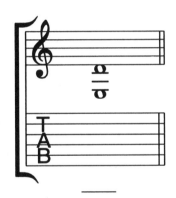

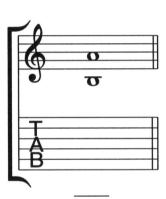

Fill in the chord frame diagrams to illustrate how the chords are fingered on the guitar fretboard:

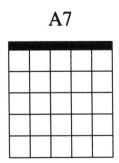

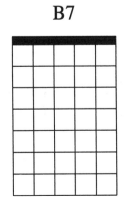

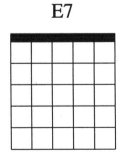

Use after page 35 of *Belwin's 21st Century Guitar Method 2*.

The Key of D

The key of D contains two sharps: F♯ and C♯.
Name the notes of the D scale. Remember there are two sharps in the key signature.

___ ___ ___ ___ ___ ___ ___ ___

The pattern of whole steps and half steps in the D scale is the same as in the C scale, the G scale and all other major scales.

Indicate if the distance between each note of the scale is a whole step (W) or half step (1/2).

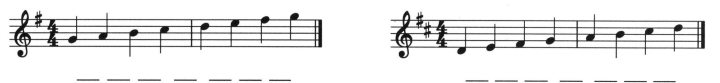

___ ___ ___ ___ ___ ___ ___   ___ ___ ___ ___ ___ ___ ___

Indicate on the fingerboard, the place where each note of the D scale would be played.

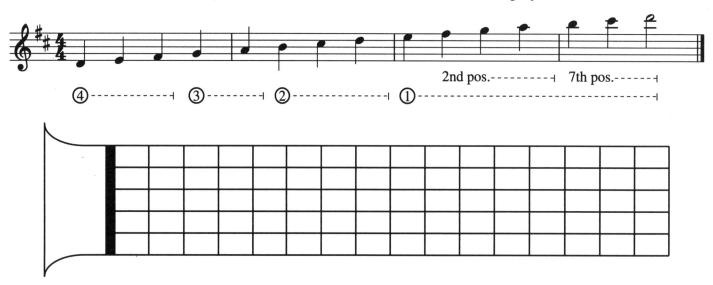

Name the notes and play them.

___ ___ ___ ___ ___ ___ ___ ___

Use after page 37 of Belwin's 21st Century Guitar Method 2.

24

As we learned in the keys of C and G, the primary chords in any key are those built on the first (I), fourth (IV) and fifth (V) degrees of the scale.

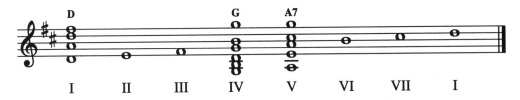

The chord built on the 1st degree of the D scale is the D chord, or I chord in the key of D.
The chord built on the 4th degree of the scale is the G chord, or IV chord in the key of D.
The chord built on the 5th degree of the scale is the A7 chord, or V7 chord in the key of D.

The D, G and A7 chords are illustrated on the chord frame diagrams. Draw the indicated notes on the music staff.

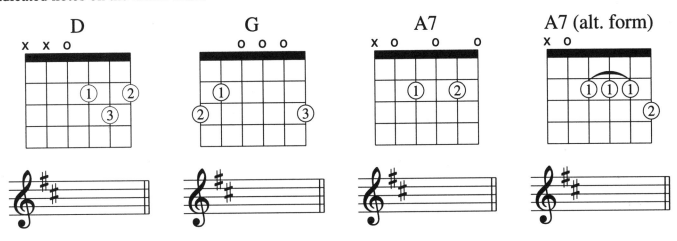

1. Notate, on the tablature, the chords indicated on the staff.
2. Name the chords and indicate the Roman numeral that shows their relationship to the key of D.

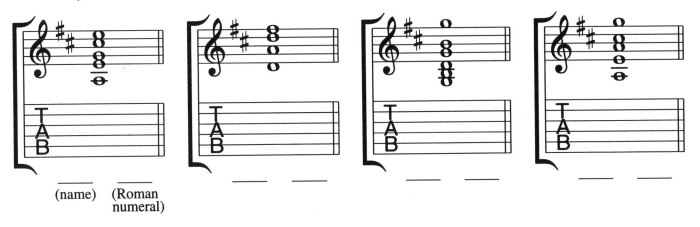

(name)   (Roman numeral)

Use after page 38 of Belwin's 21st Century Guitar Method 2.

In the keys of C and G we learned the most used secondary chords were II and VI. For the key of D we'll add one more secondary chord, the III chord (F♯m).

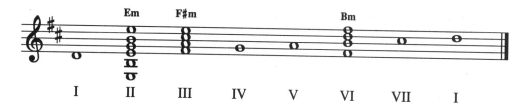

The chord built on the 2nd degree of the D scale is the Em chord, or II chord in the key of D.
The chord built on the 3rd degree of the scale is the F♯m chord, or III chord in the key of D.
The chord built on the 6th degree of the scale is the Bm chord, or VI chord in the key of D.

1. Notate, on the tablature, the chords indicated in the treble staff.
2. Name the chords.

Fill in the chord frame diagrams to illustrate how the chords are fingered on the guitar fretboard and indicate the Roman numeral that shows their relationship to the key of D.

Em

F♯m

Bm

Use after page 39 of *Belwin's 21st Century Guitar Method 2.*

Fill in the chord frame diagrams to illustrate how the chords are fingered on the guitar fretboard:

A7 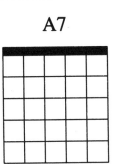   A7 (alt. form) 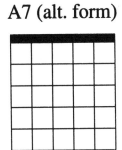   D 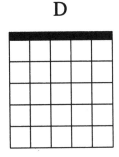   G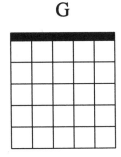

The F♯m, Bm and Em chords are illustrated on the chord frame diagrams below. Fill in the notes on the music staff.

F♯m 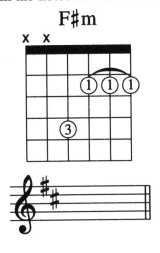   Bm 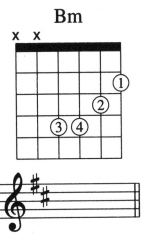   Em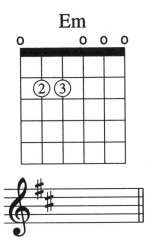

1. Write the chords indicated by the Roman numerals for the key of D.
2. Notate the chords on the tablature.

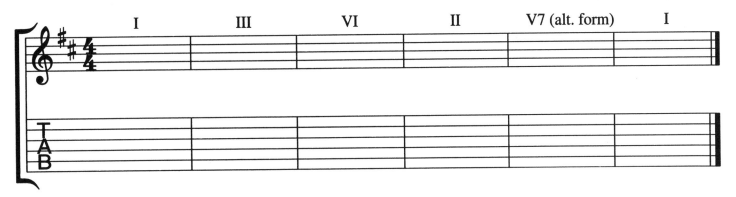

I   III   VI   II   V7 (alt. form)   I

3. Name the chords and play them.

Use after page 39 of Belwin's 21st Century Guitar Method 2.

27

The 2nd Position

1. **In first position,** notate, on the tablature, the notes indicated on the treble staff.
2. Fill in the fingering numbers.
3. Play the example.

1. **In second position,** notate, on the tablature, the notes indicated on the treble staff (the same as the previous example).
2. Fill in the fingering numbers.
3. Play the example.

In second position, indicate on the fingerboard the place where each note of the music would be played (use no open strings).

Use after page 42 of *Belwin's 21st Century Guitar Method 2.*

The A and E7 chords are illustrated in the following chord frame diagrams. Draw the indicated notes on the music staff.

A
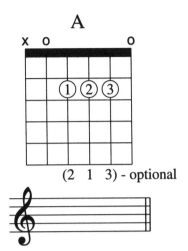

(2   1   3) - optional

E7
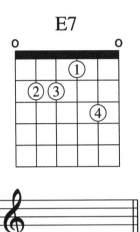

1. Notate, on the tablature, the chords indicated in the treble staff.
2. Name the chords.

2nd Position Review

1. In second position, notate on the tablature the notes indicated in the treble staff.
2. Fill in the fingering numbers.
3. Play the example.

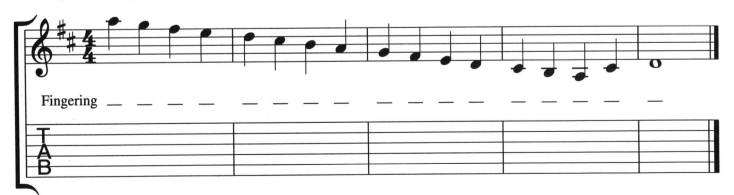

Fingering

Use after page 43 of *Belwin's 21st Century Guitar Method 2.*

On page 22 of this theory book we outlined and played *The Blues Shuffle* in E. *The Groove Shuffle* follows the same form in A, with a different rhythm pattern.

The Groove Shuffle

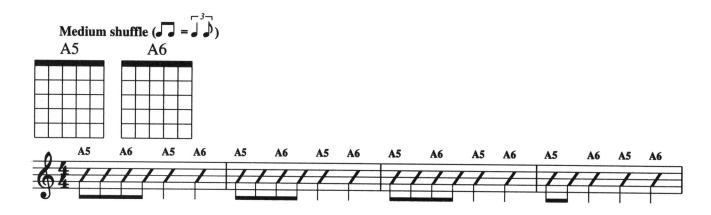

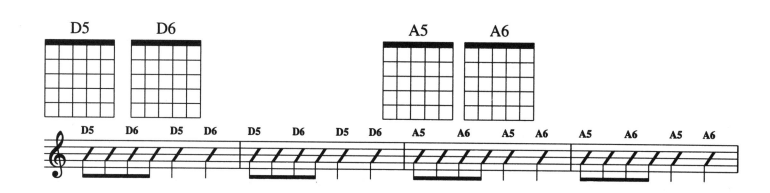

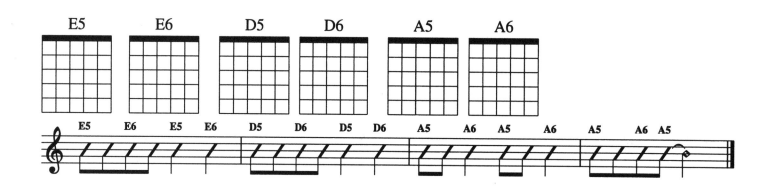

Use after page 44 of *Belwin's 21st Century Guitar Method 2*.

Indicate the correct fingerings at the correct frets to complete this chord chart.

A
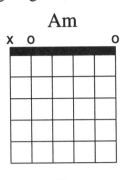

Am
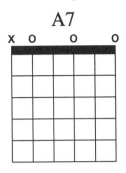

A7
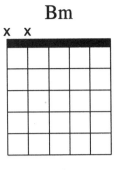

Bm
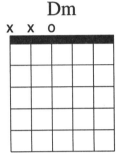

B7
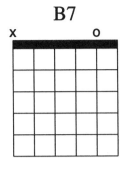

C
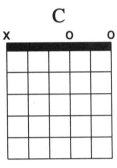

D
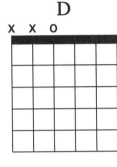

Dm
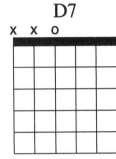

D7

Em
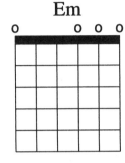

E7
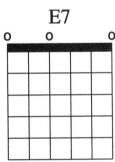

F
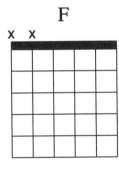

F#m
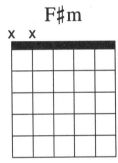

G
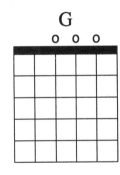

G7
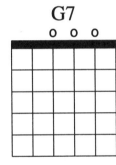

Power Chords

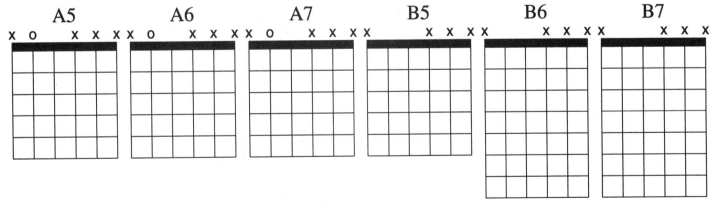

A5   A6   A7   B5   B6   B7

D5
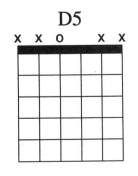

D6
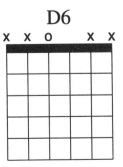

E5
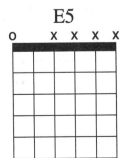

E6
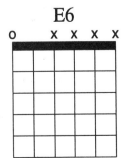

E7
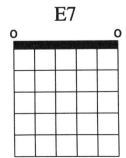

Guitar Fingerboard Chart

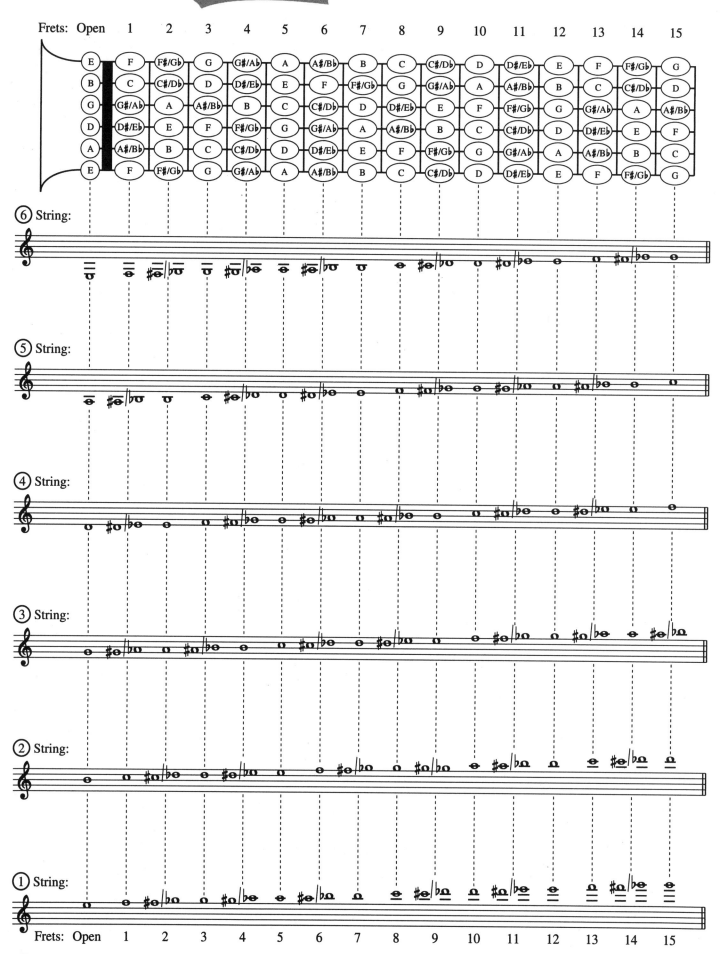